Alabama

Southern Messenger Poets
Dave Smith, Series Editor

Alabama

poems

RODNEY JONES

LOUISIANA STATE UNIVERSITY PRESS
BATON ROUGE

Published by Louisiana State University Press
lsupress.org

LSU Press Paperback Original

DESIGNER: Michelle A. Neustrom
TYPEFACES: Fournier MT Pro, text; Acumin Variable Concept, display

Grateful acknowledgement is made to the editors of the following publications, in which some
of these poems appeared previously: *Academy of American Poets Poem-A-Day*, the *American
Journal of Poetry*, *Arts & Letters*, the *Atlantic Monthly*, the *Best American Poetry 2022* (eds.
Matthew Zapruder and David Lehman), *Birmingham Poetry Review*, *Blackbird*, *Christianity &
Literature*, *Five Points*, *Kenyon Review*, *LEON Literary Review*, *Literary Matters*, the *Maple Leaf
Rag Anthology 2019*, *New England Review*, *New Ohio Review*, *Oxford American*, *Poetry*, *Poetry
Daily*, *River Styx*, *Scoundrel Time*, the *Southern Poetry Anthology, Volume X: Alabama*, *The
Southern Review*, the *Threepenny Review*.

A special thanks for help on early drafts of poems to my friends in the New Orleans
workshop started by Peter Cooley twenty years ago: Kathleen Balma, Allison Campbell, Peter
Cooley, Toi Derricotte, Carolyn Hembree, Kay Murphy, Laura Mullen, Brad Richard, and
Andy Young. Thanks also Laurie Rosenblatt, Adrian Blevins, James Kimbrell, Kerry James
Evans, and Sam Maisel for comments on several versions of the manuscript.

Cover illustration courtesy istockphoto.com/IlyaAMT.

LIBRARY OF CONGRESS CATALOGING-IN-PUBLICATION DATA
Names: Jones, Rodney, 1950– author.
Title: Alabama : poems / Rodney Jones.
Description: Baton Rouge : Louisiana State University Press, [2023] |
    Series: Southern messenger poets
Identifiers: LCCN 2022058690 (print) | LCCN 2022058691 (ebook) |
    ISBN 978-0-8071-8010-5 (paperback) | ISBN 978-0-8071-8056-3 (pdf) |
    ISBN 978-0-8071-8055-6 (epub)
Subjects: LCGFT: Poetry.
Classification: LCC PS3560.O5263 A73 2023 (print) | LCC PS3560.O5263
    (ebook) | DDC 811/.54—dc23/eng/20221213
LC record available at https://lccn.loc.gov/2022058690
LC ebook record available at https://lccn.loc.gov/2022058691

for Katy

No one can be an atheist who does not know all things.
Only God is an atheist. The devil is the greatest believer
& he has his reasons.

—FLANNERY O'CONNOR

About a Quarter Pound of Bologna

Our butcher was not fond of measure—
good at it, but not fond of it—
brandishing what technique
he had taken from his father
with deft slices through pink
balloons of meat. No one
argued the number he
jotted on the wrapping paper.
To insist he buy a scale would seem an act
of violence against his ancestors.
It was a small town. There were
no tall men in town. There
were tall women and they
were aware of the shortage.

Contents

Alabama

I Live I Live I Live

The night after the last infusion
I dream of stealing an airplane,
a single-engine, yellow Piper Cub,

and I should tell you right now
before I forget, it is a great boon
to dream of stealing an airplane after chemotherapy.

I follow the L&N tracks
south toward Birmingham, a windy day,
and after the square green fields

of Limestone County,
as I'm floating through the blue mists
of the Sand Mountain Plateau

I realize I've never actually landed.
But what a rush to sit on air
overlooking the Mulberry River.

I am in the sweet spot,
the part of earth
most directly situated

beneath heaven. I adore
the smell of grease! And then
morning, I'm sitting

in my red pajamas, eating
pancakes with strawberries.
I am better than I was on Friday,

and the next day, Sunday,
no fever, I am back!
I feel like orange juice and toast.

When the phone rings,
perhaps it's the bendamustine
that makes me greet you,

"Hurry, darling. Come.
The air smells like grape leaves.
Pack your snoods."

All human time is simultaneous. Here it is 1980. I am in a Santerismo séance in San Juan, but I came with a lawyer. Until I see the feathers and bones and the holograph of a smirking Jesus, the medium is a judge and we are in night court. Here it is 2016 in New Orleans. I live with Katy in the Faubourg Delassize opposite a brownfield that was once the Saratoga incinerator, and three retired cemeteries. At night the city over there, which, close up, reeks of the vomit of beggars and celebrities, shines from thousands of lit windows.

Maurice Merleau-Ponty writes that each time we see a new image it changes our perceptions of everything that came before. The view of the city changes 1952. The first year I feel shame. I am running toward the outhouse. A neighbor woman, Modena Hardin, is bathing me in a porcelain dishpan. Shame is feeling that the place is watching.

He Said She'd Have to Walk Six Miles
to Draw Them Water

Willodean wore long-sleeved black shirts
and long dresses with her hair swept back

from her face and falling down her back
clean to the waist in a straight braid,

she and the sisters always in black
according to the strict proscriptions

of their father, the old man in suspenders
and beard, who had peculiar ways,

people said, living like that, up in a hollow
between Nebo and Mount Zion. A cult,

some had it, of one family, the old man Will
and his daughters: Willodean, the painter;

Wilma, the philosopher; and Willa, the singer.
Some told of a wife who died in childbirth,

two sons disowned and driven off like lion cubs.
Though few saw the family in their daily life,

holding to the old ways, in holy abstinence.
They hoed, they sewed, they milked the cows.

Some Saturdays they would ride to town
and sell produce from the back of a wagon:

preserves, honey, lettuce, watermelons;
and handiworks: footstools and whatnots,

woolen socks, and Willodean's paintings:
a goat in a churn, a crawfish with sextant,

smoke boiling up from a fleeing animal.
Daubed onto bedsheets—few bought them.

But then, briefly, her name was everywhere,
the paintings in museums, everyone had to have one.

This happened as horses disappeared,
as the Beatles harmonized on Ed Sullivan,

before the depot became the bistro.
When a troglodyte on public television discussed

Willodean's technique with chiaroscuro,
he said it was as if a genius from a remote tribe

in Borneo had discovered, by scratching in dirt,
the rudiments of Euclidian geometry.

But it is all gone now: the decoys and the whatnots,
and the strange paintings for two dollars.

No record of Willa's singing or Wilma's logic.
Like nuns or crows, a girl said, and it was true.

To see them, who'd know one from the other?
Once an expert came to Saturday market

to ask Willodean questions. She never spoke.
The old man Will spoke for her. These paintings,

he said, were part of prophecy. She saw, but did
not seek these visions, and he said the blasting

had started on the bluffs, Judgment Day
was coming. The interstate would be a sign.

Small houses about a quarter of a mile apart, of whitewashed or unpainted clapboard, each with a well and outhouse, a few with barns, chicken coops, toolsheds, and smokehouses. My people are homemakers and small farmers, mainly self-sufficient. Neither much money nor light has arrived, most neighbors sign X, and, for every six automobiles, there comes a horse-drawn wagon, often trailed by a skittish and ungainly colt.

The shame of provenance is not genetic. It is installed like electricity.

The Death of Joshua Vinzant

They left the university and returned to the town of his birth. For her, five sections of comp. For him, carpentry again, rehabbing old houses.

A part of the story late one night years before they met, he called. I could hear the outrageous drunken happiness of a woman splashing near him in the pool, and though he knew I would not come over, he loved me enough to want me at the very least to talk to her.

The wife had a child already when they began seeing each other, and she knew the first night he was kind she could trust him with that boy.

He never mentioned his father.

He measured everything three times. A cheater is a butt-cut scrap or block wedged into a space between warped boards to straighten the lines. With his death he straightened a line.

He was neat even before he met her and lived in the trailer. Not a spot anywhere, everything bleached, sprayed with antiseptic.

He laughed often and without volition. When she laughed, he struck his thighs with both hands and whooped. The whoop rose from his psyche and did not come from depression or philosophy.

Among his matched set of friends who read Nietzsche and listened to the Allman Brothers not one believed him unhappy.

Closure, the heaven of positive thinkers, sometimes depends on revenge, and there is no revenge with suicides. What are you going to do? Send them to a retreat?

Crystal meth, said one friend, limits the capacity to produce dopamine, maybe that's why he did it.

He wore a butch haircut and horn-rimmed glasses. To look like Buddy Holly was to switch on an amp. To fuck-up was to make people laugh.

In his favorite joke a man passes out a friend draws a penis and scrotum on his forehead and as he walks to work he is elated that everyone is smiling.

In his poems death is on every page and if not the main subject—the image, idea, or metaphor he is focused on—it stays in his actual death like the smell of the petrichor incarnated in the downpour.

With any death, not just suicides, the temptation of the living to feel that the death is their fault plays to the heart of narcissism.

I felt culpable. I was his teacher.

Once she had their own child, he helped with the late feedings and the diapers—he did not prefer *his* son.

When we drank alone together, he drifted inward. He flickered, dimmer and dimmer—he never angered—he went out slowly like a fire.

One day a letter arrived. She had received a fellowship. To celebrate he bought himself a truck.

When he wrote me that he spent his nights driving county roads, drinking Jack Daniels and shooting feral cats, he wrote it like a joke.

Convicted the third time of DUI he was sentenced to home arrest.

The GPS anklet chafed—"Why not just pay a veterinarian to insert a chip?" he said.

One morning he went out to a shed, tied a rope to a crossing piece, made a noose, slipped it over his head, tightened it around his neck, climbed onto a bucket, and decided.

And if he woke in paradise, blushed, and looked off to the side?

Her weeks searching for him, checking the closet, as if he might still be there hidden among empty suits, waiting to spring out and kiss her.

Months later when I called she talked of going forward: completing her research, the kids growing. I had gathered some quotes from Darwin. When birds mate for life and one dies, "a new partner is generally found on the succeeding day." I sat on Darwin like an egg.

Working hard to imagine her feelings: the prickles coming back through the numbness of the shock: lesson plans, papers, tests. Loving him, knowing he had killed the one she loved.

That habit he had of bending slightly and holding his hand over his mouth to laugh. And how long would it take, convincing him to get serious about being dead?

When Everything Is Nothing

I imagine a shirt, no thread, but I see a shirt.
Without question of having sufficient art or cloth.

But one stitch, and there I go, the shirt
forming before me, and sometimes a month

eclipsed by the design of a pocket or a resolution
to take on some difficult taper I've avoided

or let go of patterns I've needlessly repeated.
I could say it is perfect. Unfinished. Unstarted.

I hold it and do not hold it, the pure notion
of the collar, lapel, sleeves, and pearl buttons.

Then I am transported, as to a gigantic fish-fry.
The shirt that will never be and the shirt

that was and does not remain are the same.
I see it because it is not. Absence requires music.

If there is something to show me nothing,
it is like whistling, I must make it out of air.

Here I am in a cotton field north of the house. One of the pickers, a woman with red hair who just got out of the pen, is saying, "I'd rather kill a man than a dog." My mother is an unhappy field boss. My father is away, painting houses to earn money to buy more land. A boy tells me that if a rattlesnake bites me I will die, but if a rattlesnake bites him, he will live. He has the holy ghost. Now the field is empty except for my mother, my sister, and me. My mother has caught a man at the scale with rocks in his sack, and when she fires him, the other pickers decamp in solidarity.

A dirt road in front of our house stretches along the side of the mountain. To the west downhill around a curve it passes the old Jones schoolhouse, which was turned into a residence when the county consolidated the schools. I am bored. There are only tattling, Christian girls to play with. When they send me out to shop, I sneak up the road and eavesdrop at the bootlegger's.

The Worst Thing Ever Done to Me

I was four—what did I know?—
playing on the front porch.

Early spring.
The mimosa was in bloom.
Eisenhower was in the White House.

Usually when I played, I became a car,
the noises of the engine,
the clutch, and the tires
scorching around corners.

Or my body was a car—my mind drove.

Twilight, a little before supper.
My father, just home from work,
was talking with a neighbor—
a bachelor cousin,
a farmer and minister.

A beautiful little knot
nearly everyone treated like a saint
for the fervor of his prayers
and his epic sermons
on the black children of Cain.

Do not suppose I am not grateful
the worst thing ever done to me
did not involve boiling water,
electricity, bullwhip, pliers,
starvation, pruning shears, ax,
chain, blackmail, blow job, or rope.

I was not doped or blown up.
I was not snuffed in a hole.

For the crime of interrupting
a conversation about guano
by mimicking the noise
of an old car backfiring,
I was lifted by the ears
and swung like a pig.

I did not scream. I swung,
hurt and confused—what

else could I do? Slip off
my ears like sandals? Channel
Jehovah and smite the preacher
into perdition?

While my father procrastinated
a millisecond,
our three-legged dog
deus ex machina
sprang up from the yard
to save me.

I am not saying
it was not justice
to see him,
the beautiful little knot,
grabbed by the throat,
brought down and squirming
as he prayed
to my father to call off the dog.

I am not saying it was not righteous.

There were still
a few minutes of light
darkening in the mimosa.

I could hear chicken frying,
then the noise of the cold
engine turning over—

again. Again. Again,
and I started. I ran.
I sang "Earth Angel," softly.

My father often tells of meeting a cousin, John Jones, who studied classics at Columbia before returning home to farm. They are standing in downtown Cullman and John says, in front of the women and the children, "Goddam, I would have been so much better off if I hadn't been born in Cullman County." When my father tells us, he spells out G-o-d-d-a-m.

Two Heroes of Love

Aloof all his life, an assistant
on his brother's dairy farm
good on the tractor and with cows—
when Knox met Savannah she
was twice widowed. Her youngest son,
61, three years his senior.
That first year neighbors whispered,
the way they rode together in the pickup,
the old lady, who looked like Gertrude Stein,
and the handsome, middle-aged gentleman,
spooning like teenagers:
a disturbance, a mild
displacement of the ideal.
Some said *peculiar,* others, *queer.*
After a while, the strangeness wore off.
Why do I think of them now?
I hardly knew them,
their brief, unlikely marriage
in a trailer behind a water tank:
a black and white television,
a plug of tobacco, a dip of snuff,
and the adoration of the pickup.
When she died I would see him again
with that truck, bending
under the hood he'd waxed and buffed
to set the points and change the plugs.

Wherever I go in Alabama, the story follows. The form of the story is a mystery, for it is not exactly handed down, but added to and subtracted from and totaled differently by each citizen as the sum and account, so that it can be further revised and debated. If one finds in a pasture a pistol clotted with dirt and corrosion, in the story it will be reunited with its owner: first as the toy of a dead second cousin, then as the real pistol of a man named Quattlebaum. Over that same pasture, during the Second World War, as a plane passes over, a leather satchel drops. James Hardin, cleaning his fence-line, thinks bomb and sprints for cover.

I am timid like James Hardin. My sister is all outward energy. She leads. In the nineties she stands up to the Vulcan Corporation and stops a quarry. Here, she sits me in a high chair, smears bacon grease over my head, and prepares to cut my hair. In 2008 I am giving a poetry reading with Ellen Bryant Voigt at the Library of Congress. When Charles Simic, the poet laureate, introduces me, he mentions peasant poets. A year later in Chattanooga when I am inducted into the Fellowship of Southern Writers, Ellen introduces me as a peasant poet. On one hand, I am pleased. On the other, I prefer "postmodernist outdoorsman."

To Kill a Mockingbird

At the beginning of sixth grade
when I learned that a man,
Mr. Key, was to be my teacher,
I was dismayed. Mrs. Anders,
the other sixth grade teacher,
with whom I was in love,
was pretty and efficient
and had taught my sister
who had never made a B.
And, also, I possibly assumed,
teaching, like giving birth,
was a thing men did not do.
Plus, Mr. Key was old. He slept
a lot. He spat tobacco juice
into a tin beneath his desk.
While we, his students, conjugated
to lie and *to lay*, or endured
unending division, he read
The Wall Street Journal. He left
often, for he was also Principal,
and each time he left, my friend,
Pete Petty, would kneel, chuckle,
and start to gnaw on my shoulder.
I do not know why he did that.
He was not predatory, but would not
stop when asked; he persisted,
chewing deeper, leaving tooth marks
until, one day, resolved to end it,
I took the football I always carried,
and just as I brought it down
on Pete's head, hello Mr. Key!
But no expression on his face, no
sign that soon each morning Pete
would be cranking the flag

up the pole, and in the afternoon
lowering it, walking inside, folding it
into a perfect triangle and laying
it in a cabinet. My punishment
was reading, alone in his office
an hour and a half after lunch,
reading *To Kill a Mockingbird*.
And he never explained why
this book, its plots and themes.
I thought of the death penalty—
I thought of it again and again—
and then Mr. Key would return
with bucket, soap, water, and rag
and make me kneel in the bathroom
and scrub graffiti from the wall
above the toilet, saying I would
need to learn these words, too,
coming from a Christian home,
a country boy, but college material.

1976 I am teaching the sonnet to high school juniors. One says, "We can't do this. It's too hard. We're not from New York. We're from Alabama."

A Hippie in Alabama

Reading Tolstoy's Christian pacifist books
and a Rand McNally map of Canada,
I had taken summer work, second shift
in a copper tubing factory, a posh job—

I stood at a saw, tubes approached—chop chop—
fat rings clinked in a bin. But like it was folded
in a book, the 6' 4" foreman on my shoulder
shouting "faster!" and Irv, the forklift guy,

whispering, "Easy, honey. We do this all year."
Driving home through cotton fields
to write with careful urgency,
in my journal: *I was paralyzed in the dilemma.*

Some nights I see myself as Simone Veil.
But I had made nearly a hundred dollars.
When I learned the rings I cut
were obturating rings for mortar shells,

I was horrified. I do not remember
when I learned, whoever told me. Like
Westmoreland, I counted bodies.
30,000 times a night I mashed a button.

In Neverland

The mine heals. The black widow crawls away
From the sleeve of my father's coveralls.
The beaten woman retrieves her maiden name.

Permission of the deepest sort—freedom
From tasks, from debts, from guilt, from love—
Is no longer the exclusive realm of husbands.

The pilot passes high beyond the wedding
And drops his bombs in the desert.
The man in the orange windbreaker

With the knife in his gym bag knocks,
But the retired teacher expecting the nice
Young reporter who writes articles on chanterelles

Hears only the whistle of her teapot,
Rushes to the kitchen, and does not answer the door.

The trees are in their autumn beauty. The woodland paths are dry, but within a mile of here over a period of forty years these victims. Glenn Lanningham shot six times on the steps of his girlfriend's house. Her ex-husband, who had recently gotten out of the army, laying for him in the shadows with a .22 rifle. Venetia Wilheit, a cousin, and her two children held hostage for hours by the father. A bungalow just up the road surrounded by police. A little after midnight, the kids escaped. But straightaway he killed her, then himself, with a Saturday night special bought at a gun show in Nashville. The oldest boy is still not right. Billy Joe Powell, the shy electrician with the pretty wife, had told his priapic asshole of an uncle not to come back. When he came back, Billy shot him. Two buckshot to the belly from a .12-gauge. The judge went easy on him. Third-degree murder—a sentence of 18 months. He didn't last a year. Leukemia. Two brothers: Jerry Hardin, who, as a boy liked to take apart watches, and could fix anything, well-liked, even after he came back from Vietnam a heroin addict; and the older, Wilburn, good at math—he ran a reputable body shop and married a teacher. Both drunk as eternity, fishing in their daddy's pond. A drowning. The older. The younger blacked out. I imagined smoke coming up from a tire they had burned to stay warm, and on the stringer in the shallow water a nice mess of catfish. I wondered, Did the man who found the dead man fry them in his skillet, or let them go? I thought of a number of things. Any image that made me care less. The beauty of goldenrod in neglected fields. Swann's peace of mind as he finally detaches from Odette. The more we care the more dangerous we get.

June 16, 2016

I am listening to talk radio as I drive home to visit my mother
Who has Alzheimer's and is in a diabetic coma,
A hot day, orange barrels dividing
The bumpy lane I am driving on from the smooth black one
Where the workers are moving back and forth on pavement rollers.
One of the drivers wears earphones.
He is smiling and nodding.
Perhaps he is listening to the same station,
Which makes me rigid with anger because I am a Democrat
And from Tuscaloosa to Bessemer they have been discussing the issue
Of Obama's being born in Africa and not America,
And just after I've turned north in Birmingham
A man calls from South Carolina to say he remembers seeing
An early edition of Obama's first book, *Dreams from My Father*,
And it was printed right there, plain as daylight
On the back cover, "Born in Kenya,"
Though you can't find those copies anymore.
Those copies have all been destroyed.
And as I'm passing through Fultondale
Another listener pipes in from North Dakota
To say he saw that cover too, and why doesn't some reporter
From the *New York Times* or the *Washington Post* report that
Instead of writing lies about Trump,
And this is where my car blows up.
Or to be more precise, the engine seizes,
Nothing when I press the gas pedal
So all I can do is pull off to the side, step out,
Go around, lift the hood, and sniff for chemicals
That might signal *oil pump* or *relay switch*
Instead of *thrown rod* or *cracked block*,
But all the time wondering if it's possible
For rage, and I mean a really substantial moral rage,
To pass from a man's fingers into a Japanese car
As the demons in the holy scripture passed into the swine.

Though, of course, cars, even American cars, do not have souls.
My car, which is eleven years old, has overheated.
And now, as is my practice when upset, I impose a curfew
On any ideas that do not directly relate to "now."
Also, I attempt to name the elements in the periodic table,
And, as I wait for the wrecker, I look down the right-of-way
To the parking lot of a Nazarene church. A man in a yellow cap
Is selling watermelons out of the bed of a pickup truck
And though it is a hot day, from time to time a customer stops
To thump one then another until he finds the right one.
But then I am being loaded and taken back
On the bumpy lane by the orange barrels toward Birmingham.
The driver of the truck is named Aubrey.
He has a sixty-acre farm and an Allis-Chalmers tractor.
And it is a delight not to hear the name repeating,
But the man who owns the garage edifies me
Re: Martin Luther King's marchers breaking windows
And defecating on the front porches of white people.
At noon the garage is like a country store. Here
Are the deputy sheriff and his red-headed cousin, Tim.
Here the owner's son, John, who was educated as an attorney
And played minor league baseball with Colby Rasmus
Before returning to the family business to serve as manager.
For him I have some hope. As he phones
Distributors to price clutches and wheel bearings,
He is polite, deferential, and well-spoken.
But in the background I can hear the radio,
One name repeating along with Soros, Barry Soetoro,
And the notorious criminal family, the Clintons,
Before the owner says, "you'll need a remanufactured engine,
And adds, "Just wait, you'll see, he'll be elected."
Because I was taught to weigh the opinions of the other side,
I listen as I have listened to talk radio
And thought, "Someday you will laugh at this,"
But the day is sore,
And I walk to the car rental sick to death of Alabama.

Why does Fairview matter? Transformed, time-doctored, deracinated—all the houses have been wired, the road paved. Still I go back. A mastiff growls. The blind piano tuner passes with his driver. 1967 woos 1953. The life of the mind transcends the known ridges and enters the habitation of rumors. In the nearer distances live possum eaters, snake-handlers, and water-witchers. The angel of death only a few years earlier rides a white horse up this road to the house where Nancy Cooper lies dying. At the gate out front angel and horse rise into the sky, harvesting her soul. The atheist Tom Nesmith was there and he confirmed it.

Identifying with Stars

In this movie we are streaming, a winsome lass
lopes down a long meadow to a cliff above the sea.
She has been cast for her skin and her hair,
the way the warrior she will love was cast
for his eyes and the fine bones in his face,
as these rocks have been cast from all the millions
of rocks beside the sea because these rocks
have just that precise darkness the light loves.

If this had been made in 2019, we would surely be
watching something about female assassins
or the new *Sherlock Holmes*—we like both episodes
where he dies and comes back to life—
we were raised Christian, after all,
but this movie is from 1986 or '87 when everyone was dying
to see historical romances. The stars
had to be gorgeous, the scenery tall,

and if one rock was speckled with grease
or its dots of mica reflected too brightly, a double
would be brought in. Oh, I know it is just
sleight-of-heart. She will walk down the hill
and lower her bucket into a spring
eight hundred miles away, and in a New York
minute, pose in a basement in Los Angeles,

looking up into the famous lips of a short man
who stands on a box. And though Katy
is approximately my height, I will become him.
We will embody that kiss, and the war scene
where I climb out of the trench, facing the enemy,
knowing the blood on their bayonets is paint,
they are extras, not even stars, but so large
and so many, I am a little afraid they will kill me.

Because I dream I am Winston Churchill, because, in the front yard, I am never unwatched, only Sunday afternoons, in the unsurveilled hour while our parents are blithely making love, bicycle polo is played in a pine thicket on the side of the mountain. With croquet mallets and English accents. A gentlemen's sport: there are multiple injuries; hardly anyone ever scores.

Why Am I Making This Noise

With this worm and this word
I am teaching
My starling to talk
worm worm worm

I am careful to enunciate
Each word
At the exact instant
I drop the worm right

In front of her
Jigging it for emphasis
To further demonstrate
My meaning

But when she pays
No mind think no
Of course I have
Upset her she is

A vegetarian so
I find a berry they
Are not hard to find
And again I work

With two props
One berry one word
berry berry berry
I spin it as I say it

But again zero
Well I say well I will
Up the register
Starlings are

Very smart have
You never heard them
Winging together
Over a cornfield

Sometimes they will
Form an hourglass
Pour through the
Neck of the funnel

And come out
In disparate squads
Parallelograms
Hexagons and

Once in a light rain
A parasol of starlings
But all she does
Is flutter to the top

Of a mulberry
And fluff up
Maybe I am not
Her human but

Listen close wait
She is saying *ach*
ach she says *ach ach*
And though I have

No langue d'oc
I say it back *ach ach ach*
And as I say it
I clack my sallow beak

My grandparent's house and barn sit on the right and the Fairview Church of God to the left. Their house is a neat square two-bedroom house with green shutters. It stands a little in front of the concrete porch of their previous house, which burned. The church, too, is tied to disaster, as it was moved from the southwest corner of the valley after a tornado blew away the previous church. A few old men still blame the tornado on women who wear jewelry and mascara.

Heroism at the End of Middle Age

It is when I look at myself
in the mirror above the vanity
that I am transformed to Uncle Larkin

as he jaunts from the shower
after twenty-four holes of golf,
smelling beautifully of talcum;

as he engages the cruise
and glides through rolling lawns,
resplendent in yellow

blazer and lime green trousers,
in a matching Cadillac and socks.
I ride beside him, smiling

as if posing for a stamp,
and know beauty is a lie—
I do not have to become John Keats to know

the light brown curls
of my hair in the mirror
have been gray for years in photographs.

For a long time after Charlie the gelding dies and my grandfather borrows a tractor, drags his body to a little hill above the creek and buries him, Nell, the remaining half of the team, stands by the grave and screams. The moot cry of pointless opposition, in opera it is usually soprano. At the first Olympics the athletes wrestled naked so nothing would be hidden. At their son's first birthday party Jen blurts out, in front of everyone, to her husband who has hanged himself and to the gods of fate and oblivion, "Goddammit, Josh. You get to be dead. I have to be at Chuck E. Cheese."

Scatter

Often I start with the random and work
toward the inevitable,

and with the blind pleasure of one who has walked
fifty years in the wilderness, write

music with nervous system seeks
willing instrument with vine smarts.

It tickleth me. It tickleth me not.
Often I stop and pray to S'su ma Chien.

Sometimes out of sheer desperation
or superstition, I dress in a white suit.

As for clutter, I believe in leaving it alone
until I require some draft that I've lost,

or some book like *The Ponder Heart*
by Eudora Welty, which really hit me

because of that way she has of making
the most ornery people vaguely likeable.

And I think it will be difficult, this foray
into the clutter, for I will have to squat

among archipelagoes of papers that are
dog-eared and notarized by footprints

and to relocate brown recluse spiders
and collate pink and yellow receipts for tax season

while fighting the suspicion that order,
or that obsessive species of order which Freud

associated with the anal stage, is for Fascists
while I am all laissez-faire and trial-and-error,

not the messiest duck in the slough, but more
like Eudora. If you have ever visited her home,

now it is a museum with immaculate gardens,
but before she died, she decreed that books

should be dropped pell-mell all over the house.
Howard Nemerov was worse. His packet-

bollixed foyer. His kitchen dice-roll
of empty wine bottles. His dining table's

leaning book towers collapsed in a shambles.
After midnight, he paused and reached in one,

The Life of Jonathon Wild the Great,
and withdrew a royalty check from 1962.

That was transcendence, laughing from one eyebrow
while all around us the long, slow explosion

of paper, wine, and books, held still, and I saw myself,
one foot in a nest, another in a labyrinth.

I have a few ideas, and two elegies if I can find them.

The church is nondenominational. Like gravity, it holds things together. We go there three times a week to keep things from flying apart. To my mother, who was reared Methodist, the church needs finesse and a more dignified service, free of foot-washings and hollering. My mother is a philosopher. She studies and allows some gospel but does not condone Paul, whose pronouncements on marriage strike her as fanatical. She suggests to my sister and me that we should not be indoctrinated. Nevertheless, salvation, like hard work, is expected.

It is hard work not to be saved. Even a mediocre country evangelist is seasoned in the very rhetoric of the tear ducts. Like a murder ballad, he plays for teenagers. Like a lawyer, he plies the nearly innocent. While his amanuensis, an elderly pianist, chums the baptistery with "Softly and Tenderly Jesus is Calling," the region high in the back of my throat, which I have identified as the soul, starts to salt and cramp. "Do you feel the presence of the Lord?" And, on this cue, a select squad of the saved and sanctified mobilizes in my direction.

My Father's Deafness

One day the sound goes out of everything that made a noise
and from that day for him all is silence
though our lips move as ever along the rutted lanes
of familiar conversations, and when he leaves
to walk down the pasture and dynamite the stump
that blocks his creek, he tamps the charge
secure inside the roots. He does not flinch
when the stump splits and opens above fields
its quiet, thousand-ribbed umbrella of debris.
At first you cannot tell if you do not know
he is deaf, almost like he reads the waves
as they pass through him. He smiles; he nods; he's immune
to self-pity. Accepting loss with grace is subject
to a benign fraudulence or central kindness in his being.
And hadn't we always joked he was hard of hearing,
the way he'd disappear if one of us should
ask for something he did not care to give
or share an opinion he did not approve?

Martha Flowers said he had *man's disease:*
he could only hear what he wanted to hear:
cattle lowing, the clank and chuff of the John Deere,
wind in pines, rain on tin, and elderly cousins
come back on Decoration Day, asking,
Which way to the cemetery? Who is in that little grave?
Who was Anaphaster? All of us in the family ask,
What could be the reason for this unhearing:
the clangor of the machines in the factory where he
worked thirty years, the six-foot fall from the loading dock
hitting the railroad track, three days in a coma,
and when he came to, the biscuits had no taste,
he could not smell the barn. And earlier, as a child, swimming
every day in a dirty creek, and before that,

before he could remember, his mother told him,
he was sick, the measles settled in his ears.

Soon it will be forty years of going back to see him
and each time speaking through a notebook
with larger letters that he takes longer to read;
or talking to him on the caption telephone,
fearing it will mistranslate "stuck in the mud"
as "motherfucker" or delete the thing I meant.
My sister and I agree, How can we live without him?
Where has our mother, his guide and interpreter, gone?
Where her farmer who dressed like a New York playboy?
Three months shy of ninety-eight, like his father at ninety-six,
he balances his checkbook. He refuses to sell his truck.
In our argument against his driving to the mailbox,
he shifts the subject and lowers his voice
down the angry silence of the living room.
This is hard love, we children repeating *No*
while he concentrates as though he were listening
and the low, staccato music
of his breathing signals he will keep the goddam Chevrolet.

Jung explains my resistance to salvation: introverts are not joiners. I take comfort in the thief on the cross, who converts a moment before his death. Also, in my mother's brother, Bill, who had been dozing in his pew when the minister made a call for new church members to come forward. When the man next to him rose and walked to the front, Uncle Bill went along, joining the church half-asleep.

Watergate

For many in the United States the word brings a phase
when mortars in Vietnam still whistled around them
and the scandal of Nixon and his Machiavellian buds
poured from the news into their subconscious—I see
that Watergate too: the televised hearings, and in particular
one session—Sam Ervin had just asked Erlichman
or Dean or Haldeman, a long-winded, periphrastic,
left-branching question—it must have lasted
forty seconds and seemed three days before he paused
for effect, and Erlichman or Dean or Haldeman
answered: "Senator, could you please repeat the question?"
And he did, verbatim! And that is one Watergate.

But I think also of the morning my father sent me to the creek
that ran through our pasture to remove a dead calf
a flood had floated north to lodge against our water gate—
a little Guernsey heifer—I had petted her often—
Now flies buzzed around her, bloated and entangled
in the mesh—and I remember her eyes were open,
so she seemed to watch as I pulled first one leg
then another from the vines and wire that trapped her,
and pulled her to the bank through the shallow water.

Because the second water gate, which features the tender
relationship between a dead calf and a little boy,
happened twenty years before the first, in which men
break into an office complex in a hotel, I prefer its
posts and hog wire that kept cows from a neighbor's field
to the gray rows of filing cabinets that brought down a presidency.
The water pours out of the mountain and runs to the sea.
Sometimes I say it to myself, until the meanings leave.
I say *Watergate* until it is water pouring through water.

My father is disappointed when I decide I am an existentialist. He is a good Christian, I know, but am I not a good existentialist? I neither regret nor see the point of it.

Childhood Ends

I had found a stray two weeks earlier
scratching itself
in the canebrake
behind Nichols Pond,
a half-grown,
yellow feist.
It was not averse
to my liking.
Late afternoon, we dawdled,
and frolicked home
like any pups,
tracking overlapping circles
in the mud
of harrowed fields.
The corn was
beginning to sprout.

I was told I could keep the feist, but I must be responsible.

I looked at the pup;
it looked back
with beseeching modesty,
sidling and bowing,
not meeting my eyes,
but I imagined
if I spoke without guile,
using the exact tone
of its yips and barks,
it would correspond
in kind. For instance,
it might roll over, lie
on its back, wag
its tail, and lick my palm.

And sure enough,
despite the scratching,
these things happened
in the twilight
of my nearly
ungovernable
shyness: a partnership,
a pas-de-deux
of feints and dodges
undertaken
with full knowledge
that a feist is useless—
it will not rescue the perishing
or guard a house.

But then who was I?—
not yet an I; still a me,
a plot without agency,
mother-dressed
in a striped shirt
with button-up
elbow pockets,
horrified by the new hairs
in my armpits
and the blemishes
dotting my eyebrows.

In those days the feist and I often went up the mountain.

I had a new .410
single-barrel shotgun.
And what had I killed?
I had killed a vulture,
three baby flying squirrels
when I shot into a nest
high in a beech tree,

and a pine-tree in the churchyard
on a snowy day. The feist
beside me—two legionnaires,
a knight and his squire
crossing the drawbridge to a castle.

But the feist in the real world
itched and whined
as the days heated up.
Its hair fell out in patches.
The skin's red lakes
dried to scabs. Often
it ran in circles, snapping
at its tail. I could not tell
if it was trying to kill
the part that hurt
or escape. *The mange,*
my father said—*the feist*
will die, but I believed
in miraculous healing.

When my father told me to shoot the feist, I negotiated—
I delayed. Insisting
I would not, *I*
will not; even
when I stood there
in that muddy field
like a child soldier
aiming my shotgun
at a creature who trusted me
to pet it, I told myself
this happened in a story—
in the romantic edition,
I am Abraham bending
over Isaac, God
is merciful and I do not apologize.

Oh story of Alabama, you are not just my story. Story of Yaa Gyasi, Albert Murray, and Sonia Sanchez, story of Red Eagle and Hank Williams, story of Rosa Parks and E. O. Wilson, story of the Choctaw, Chickasaw, Creek, and Cherokee, story of Aretha recording "Respect" in the studio at Muscle Shoals, story it takes three women and one old man to tell, story that Everette Maddox ended, "Kiss my ass and make it well." My story grows from Biblical and folk rootstocks. It impedes the ever-encroaching money economy, for no payment can occur without an exchange also of stories. A good enough story, droned out with sufficient relish, works like a song. Its rhythms have more value than its meaning, and the slowness with which it is told adds value, for it is essentially dilatory, shade and respite from the heat of the midday sun. At sundown in the field when pay is offered, I am hungry, my back is hurting, and I would like to leave, but it is customary first to refuse the money.

Patriotism That Beautiful and Dangerous Idiocy

A great many of us agree with the proposition
the annual Fourth of July pig-roast should be permanently cancelled,

though I cannot help recalling the camaraderie
in the fifties when the women wore bonnets

and the men would bring blocks of ice in pickups
from the ice plant in Hartselle to keep the drinks cold;

the banjos and the mandolins, someone
always singing off-key at the top of their voice;

the pig hanging over the timbers glowing in the pit,
and you should know, if anyone asks, the pig

is not an actual pig. The pig is history.

But does it matter, really, where, or which animal?
In Johnson City, the pig was a lamb.

The men wore Hawaiian shirts, the women flowery mumus,
a linguistic anthropologist played a harp.

In Tuscaloosa, the pig was a goat, and Frank Allen told me
one year "the goat" was a dog rescued from the pound.

In Illinois, it was a calf. 1989, a month after the massacre
at Tiananmen Square, and a professor had invited

three Chinese graduate students. A great place
in the country with a swimming hole and rope swing.

There were two British rock stars and Jim, who owned
the farm and was a personal friend of Muddy Waters,

brought out a shotgun, a bucket of eggs, and a big
slingshot rubbered with the inner tube of a tractor tire.

The shooter would call "yolk!" and the egg rocket
high above the pasture. You only had a fraction of a second

to shoot. Only the best marksmen ever hit the egg.
And I remember one of the Chinese students—

as he took the shotgun from Jim, he was shaking
so I had to hold him steady—he shot wildly.

Perhaps he was shooting to protect some dear friend,
but the way the torque of the fear in his body

suddenly relaxed to laughter, I thought of orgasm,
no volition in the noise rising from his throat.

And in that instant, he was American,
he felt no embarrassment. He could do anything.

One Wednesday night, in a discussion of the eleventh chapter of Corinthians, our pastor mentions that not all Christians are saved in churches. He describes one woman's second birth in a corncrib. A few Wednesdays later, he declares that tonight each member of the congregation is to testify how long and under what conditions they have been saved, then drop one penny in the offering plate for each year that they have been a Christian. One by one, the members stand, speak, and go to sit beside him in the choir. Alone in the pews, considering the strategies of Mark Twain, I rise and walk to the altar. "I was saved in the woods behind the house a year ago," I witness and drop my penny.

In the Living Room after Dinner

Mother off her meds, stuck in deep dementia,
Chanting "We'll understand it by and by,"
And Daddy, deaf for years, talking about her
As if she weren't right there listening.
He would say, "She's not here anymore."
Then add, "We had sixty-five good years."
The television talking to no one. The curtains drawn.
The thermostat set on 81.
Then she entered the hypersexual phase.
If it shocked and embarrassed us,
It was nearly a relief to hear her moaning
Like a porn star, though her friends claimed
It was not her; it was the devil himself,
Not our mother with her hands down her pants,
Squirming, crying, "give it to me." And worse,
Behaving like this during the minister's visit.
And worse still, that conversation with Lisa,
Her caregiver, who ushered her into the bath:
Lisa: "What would your husband think?"
Mother: "I don't have a husband."
Lisa: "What would God think?"
Mother: "*God* never had it like that."
Should I be ashamed we both laughed?
That was how we knew her, by her wit.
The television was on, the curtains drawn.
In the next phase, she didn't know anyone.

The Things of This World I Looked for
I Did Not See

Not noticing is like noticing
in a way—but "no—not that way,"

mother would often say, *sotto voce*,
in the intimacy of a hide switching.

One idea being I was bad,
another that I was bad because

I was a child, and, with time,
might get better. I didn't.

I kicked a hole. I bit a Christian.
I majored in Möbius Dick.

This is why I gaze fondly into space:
I enjoy not paying attention.

I would draw nudes of accountants
with anteaters, but I lack the talent.

Still I may invent a new field: Trance Studies—
I have a small gift for infinity.

I am not bad because I am old
I am bad because I am no longer a child.

In 1965, I renounce public prayer. Briefly, I identify as a Druid: I pray to trees.

Trying to Believe /
We Are Endangered

I go inside the wolf
9:35 Sunday morning
Inside my beastly stinking
I kneel and light
A candle for snow
On the website
Churchoftheend.org

Late Monday stuck in traffic
I stick also to the wolf
Like teaberry gum
Glommed to the sole of a boot
Marked down in the Goodwill
Or ice clinging to a leaf
Three million years ago

Though I am not famished
Nor does my fur bristle
Tuesday I go inside the wolf
Following standard sheep
Of no particular breed
Maybe old testament sheep
Maybe apocalyptic statistics

How large my teeth and ears
How wild my panting Wednesday
When I put on the head
And stare out of the wolf
The Krewe of Oak jerks
And turns the corner
From Oak onto Carrollton

Hello fossils Hello Thursday
That smells like money
Hello American elm Hello dodo
Hello polar bear snoozing in a sauna
I hear inside the wolf
The Carborundum of coal drills
Resonating from glaciers

On Friday I write *Wolf Hell*
On the bank I write it in wolf blood
To make (myself) believe
The condition is critical
I donate my body to science
To synch with the wolf
And spare the cost of the funeral

Saturday crossing the causeway
Seeing three boys on skis
And sometimes in the sky
The letters of an ad or proposal
I am happy to be a rich animal driving
A great storm is coming
A tempest an uproar a furor a gah—

How Much I Loved This Life

I lay in the dark afraid of the dark,
Once, in Alabama, in 1954,
The year before electricity,
And prayed and could not pray

One lamp for all the world
And, listening, heard the L&N
Screech at Lacon, and then
The unmuted spirit breathing of the house.

I lay in the dark afraid of the dark
And thought of the word *eternity*
And of the hydrogen bomb.
Sometimes now in sleep I ululate.

When Katy shakes me, asking why,
I mean to keep things light. I say,
"That is the noise I always make
When I am being devoured."

Thank you electricity: convivial brightnesses, hot and cold running water, ovens, heaters, well-pumps, refrigerators. Where once they played Rook with neighbors, now my parents sit up late, listening to radio dramas and country music. My father wires our barn. My mother watches As the World Turns. In New York, John Cage writes Indeterminacy; in a village in Nigeria, Georgia Yorama discovers, above her husband's grandmother's bed, a signed photograph of Dolly Parton. In El Salvador at the New Year's party, the fishermen dance to Herbie Hancock's Headhunters. The titles fade from books. Our toothbrushes come from China. The very chickens we eat are strangers.

In a Dream of Chivalry

My father is helping the Ledoux sisters
move their old refrigerator
into the basement when they buy the new one.
The dolly hasn't been touched for years,
but it still has grease in the wheel bearings
and makes a mollifying squeak
as he bumps across the threshold
from the kitchen to the parlor.
He moves delicately to keep the balance,
avoiding the soft places in the floor,
and as he moves, those Ledouxs tsk
and fuss about what to fix for supper.
He thinks now on hot afternoons
as they cool off in the basement
they won't have to climb the stairs
to freshen two glasses with iced tea.
He is happy they have patched things up
after decades of not speaking.
Nina Totenberg is talking on public radio.
Pea their green parakeet is singing.
At the stairs he loosens the straps,
takes the refrigerator off the dolly,
lays it on a quilt and edges it slowly.
It is a kind day, breezy and mildly warm.
My father is not jousting or scaling a battlement.
He is watching the Ledoux sisters
show off their new refrigerator, its four adjustable
trays, chill drawer, and ice-maker—
and sees himself handsome, a knight, a sir.
Under his overalls' armor, his tie is still knotted.
A Sunday. How clean things are.
When Belle touches the button
of the little spigot on the door
clear water pours into a silver cup.

When I say I take Kafka into my heart, I mean I had a gun, but I did not shoot the television. When I say nonfiction, I mean everything is true but language.

The Manufacturing of Copper Tubing Has Changed Very Little in the Past 70 Years

and my grandparents' farm with the two draft horses,
seven milk cows, eight hogs, three kinds of chickens,
twenty-four barn cats, two-and-a-half acre garden,
six apple trees and four peach trees
dispersed across a field of sorghum,
two cornfields and three cotton patches,
is worked the same as in the thirties.
A creek still runs through it, flooding the pasture in spring,
starving to a few malnourished pools in late July.
A noon swim leaves a film of muddy sweetness.
My grandfather robs bee trees and keeps
three hives, painted white behind the garden,
so there is always honey.

Shall I compare thee, copper tubing factory, to my grandparents' farm?
Both fallow, the factory closed and repurposed,
the farm rows ploughed under and seeded for pasture.
Both the copper tubing factory and the farm cover forty acres
though the factory does not feature
a twenty-year-old roan mare who mischievously opens the gate
and trots proud as a felon to the front yard
to dine on the sweet clusters of fruit
that hang from the mulberry tree,
and on the farm you will not discover
a piercing mandrill or an engineer who knew Adolph Hitler.

The factory has three departments: casting, drawing, and finishing.
The farm has three seasons: planting, growing, and harvesting.
Copper ingots are unloaded from the train and taken to the furnace.
Bags are unloaded from a truck and seeds planted in the field,
but first my grandmother sits on the cultivator
in her calico bonnet, calling *gee* and *haw* to the team;

and at supper time, unsnaps the traces,
releases them from the single-tree, and they walk
home ahead of her; they know the way, they do not dally.

But I must tell you, as my body is hoeing in their garden,
I cannot feel the *élan vital* that brings my grandparents joy,
And my soul goes wandering through the atrium of a grand hotel
This plot of beets and onions circles like an eddy,
Even when I am swarmed by wasps and stung so many times
They have to lay me in a tub and ice me like a salmon.
Why do I think I am better than what I hate and will miss?
Enduring slow time, swapping instead of buying,
And knowing trees, shape notes, and the names of animals we eat?
Shall I come forward straightaway and admit:
It is to these pastures and fields I return to heal
When I dream the world is ending.

And in the factory as I stand at my machine,
Holding a bucking, twisting tube between two spinning metal jaws
When I look down into the gold of the copper filings
Clouding the rainbow-slick in the vat of mineral spirits,
I am not myself, but Jimi Hendrix,
Riffing "The Star Spangled Banner" with his teeth,
And I am Mary Queen of the Scots in the Tower of London,
Embroidering *"En ma Fin gît mon Commencement"*
On the cloth of her estate,
And I am Hieronymus Bosch planting *The Garden of Earthly Delights*.

Have you never asked the value of the lives you did not live?
I stand at the pointer, calculating,
and at the end of summer, my grandfather asks
how much money did you make,
and when I answer three thousand dollars,
he shakes his head, saying he has never made
even two thousand dollars a year
and never gone hungry or lacked what he needed,

though things are changing, he cannot believe
how things change. Even now it is 1969
and they are bagging manure and selling it at Walmart.

After Bird and Leona visit my grandmother in the rest home in 1990 and they pray together, she goes to the guest book and writes "colored" in parenthesis under their names. Though she has loved them all her life. She loves their voices, blent in prayer. At the church at Campground, Leona leads the singing, and Bird accompanies her. He plays fast, triplets in sixteenth notes. The one time my grandmother heard Bird play, she allowed how she preferred "a less rambunctious music." That year he would have been working nights, coming home to Chick Corea and Oscar Peterson. At Campground, when they play "Amazing Grace," the tradition is to touch every note on the piano.

All Human Time Is Simultaneous

The hours in the airplane, and the hours on the tractor,
And my parents in their dotage,
When we go back to see them.
She does not appear to know us,

And he, as if rehearsing, repeating
The same stories with the same words.
Here they are in their thirties
Walking naked through the house.

They never hid death from us. Why
Hide their bodies? Or their pride
On Sunday mornings as we watched them
Primping at the mirror for church.

Measured and ceremonious, she powders
Her cheeks and dabs her neck
With Chanel No. 5. He ties his trademark
Windsor knot. I know where they aren't,

But here in New Orleans, I search for them
As I smoke on the porch. In the space of five boards
The anole changes from viridian to ochre
And puffs out the bright red dewlap from its throat.

The common idea of Alabama shames me, but it is only an idea. The port of vision is one room, one field. Here it is 1959. Junior Flowers channels Fats Domino and Picasso. When he is not beating on a guitar, he is painting enormous, unwieldy abstractions. One day when I give him a stick of gum, he says, "I will remember you when I am famous."

Going Home

The same way each time:
the arrivals at the exit,
the turns at the closed store,
the slow short miles
through the bottoms,
after the long fast miles
up Louisiana, Mississippi, and Alabama.

The house then
the same as before: lamps
lit in every room,
the green rug,
the brass bells on shelves.
In the back bedroom
my father's grip
is of the same antiqued manliness.

But each breath shallower
and farther from the one before.
One eye has glazed over like algae,
in the other sometimes
a dim light, the torch
a lost sailor spies
through holes torn in fog.

There is little pain.
When there is, my sister
slips under his tongue
three drops of morphine.
It is bone quiet.
In the morning we are orphans.

In one year, my sister and I select two caskets. The Hardins sing at both funerals. My sister picks the songs. Rain on a night in 1958 beating on a tin door. The seven of us huddled in the storm pit listening, praying, as if we might patch the leak in infinity. And the cyclone passes.

What Will Not Be Spoken

Because I had this faint memory of the thought
of a taste in my mouth and could not name it

I went through school sad I could not say it
if I had swallowed it or was it even edible

maybe I was too young when I first had it
I did not know the word yet though the taste stayed

as I grew older some nights I could nearly
describe it and would put my tongue to chalk

and paraffin and iodine and go into grocery stores
sniffing along every aisle thinking I would find it

but I did not find it until one day when
I was not looking there it was for an instant

it came to me I said it so I would remember
though in time I forgot that is why now I write

We make five trips back to Fairview to clean house. Careful at first, we winnow the receipts, box the intimate apparel, tape names on furniture, and give hammers and gadgets to cousins, but the archive is vast. On the last trip my sister rents a dumpster. Finally, everything rolls away, but everything has been touched, and the idea follows me back to the Faubourg Delassize. Some of the packages we throw away have not been opened.

For Katy

When Milo was a kitten
and spent the night
with us in the big bed,
curled like a brown sock
at our feet, he would
wake before daybreak,
squeak plaintively
in his best Burmese,
cat-castrato soprano,
and make bread on our stomachs
until if one of us did not rise,
sleepwalk to the kitchen
and open his can of food,
he would steal under the covers,
crouch, run hard at us,
jam his head
in our armpits,
and burrow fiercely.

Probably he meant nothing by that.
Or he meant it in cat-contrary,
just as he did not intend
drawing blood the day
he bolted out the door
and was wild again
for nearly three hours.
I could not catch him
until I knelt, wormed
into the crawl space
under a neighbor house
and lured him home
with bits of dried fish.

Or he meant exactly what he smelled,
and smelled the future
as it transmogrified out of the past,
for he is, if not an olfactory
clairvoyant,
a highly nuanced cat—
an undoer of complicated knots,
who tricks cabinets,
who lives to upend tall
glasses of Merlot.
With his whole body,
he has censored the finest passages of *Moby-Dick*.
He has silenced Beethoven with one paw.
He has leapt three and a half feet
from the table by the wall
and pulled down
your favorite print by Miró.
He does not know the word no.

When you asked the vet what
kind of cat he was, she went
into the next room
came back and said,
"Havana Brown."

The yellow eyes, the voice,
the live spirit that plays into dead seriousness
and will not be punished into goodness,
but no—

an ancient, nameless breed—

mink he says and I answer in Cat.
Even if I was not

born in Birmingham
between a moldy cabbage
and an expired loaf of bread,
I too was rescued by an extravagant woman.

Effacement

In 2013 Susan Silton, the multidisciplinary artist, writes from Los Angeles for permission to use my poem "On Pickiness" in *Appraisals*, one of their projects.

As explained in the letter, they are working with pages torn out of high-end art auction catalogues and old typewriters, which intrigues me as I once collected old typewriters and wrote ad copy for billboards.

They will extract the ribbon from the typewriter, type poems that relate to issues of labor and class over captions for works of art with an ascribed value of $1 million or more, and display the pages in metal frames.

When I wrote billboards and became aware that any language passing at more than 25 mph was not being read but watched, I worked on a 1930s Smith and Corona portable.

Like *Appraisals*, "On Pickiness" is a pentimento, with a conversation between Classical revision and Romantic improvisation underlying an image of my mother picking cotton.

For the artist, typing a poem in stencil mode (without ink) across the caption for a million-dollar work of art is a form of activism. Not art you can see. A blind embossing.

One idea is that nature is a subset of artifice. I prefer the reverse. The mystery as the image emerges from the fog. The likenesses in the steady rippling of attention.

Flaubert believed that, in order for art to work, the artist must disappear.

When Howard had cancer, and I asked him why he had flown to Texas to give a reading, he answered, "Scrounging after fame and fortune."

My mother picking cotton was like Flaubert picking the right word, leaving no wispiness in the empty bolls of her perfect rows.

In *Appraisals* ten volunteers sit at a communal table, typing *Grapes of Wrath* on manual typewriters without ribbons. Behind them on a cobalt wall the thirteen appraisals have the burnished look of recently cleaned stained glass windows,

but where is "On Pickiness"?

When I submitted it to *The Atlantic* in 1995, I typed it on 100% rag content paper with the watermark, which was shaped like the earth, centered at the top, so the title would fall across the equator.

Notes

The first two sentences of "The trees are in their autumn beauty" quote
W. B. Yeats's poem "The Wild Swans at Coole."

The title "The Manufacturing of Copper Tubing Has Changed Very
Little in the Past 70 Years" is the first sentence of "How Is Copper
Tubing Made," by Andrew Jay Saxsma. My poem is for Wendell Berry.

"Trying to Believe / We Are Endangered" is in memory of E. O. Wilson.

Untitled sections are for my sister, Vondalyn Jones Hall, and my friend
Peter Cooley.

About the Author

Rodney Jones grew up on a subsistence farm in Alabama, and attended the University of Alabama and at the University of North Carolina at Greensboro. His eleven books of poetry include *Transparent Gestures* (1989), winner of the National Book Critics Circle Award; *Things That Happen Once* (1996), a finalist for the Los Angeles Times Book Award; *Elegy for the Southern Drawl* (1999), a Pulitzer finalist; and *Salvation Blues* (2006), which won the Kingsley Tufts Prize and was shortlisted for the Griffin International Poetry Prize. His other honors include the Frederick Brock Prize from *Poetry*, the Theodore Roethke Prize from *Poetry Northwest*, the *Kenyon Review* Award for Literary Excellence, the Jean Stein Prize from the American Academy of Arts and Letters, NEA and Guggenheim fellowships, and a Marfa residency from the Lannan Foundation. His work has won two Pushcart prizes and been selected for ten editions of *Best American Poetry*. In 2008 he was elected to the Fellowship of Southern Writers, and in 2016, he was inducted into the Alabama Writers Hall of Fame. He has taught at Southern Illinois University at Carbondale and the Warren Wilson low residency MFA program, served as the Mary Rodgers Field Distinguished University Professor at Depauw University, and as the Visiting Elliston Poet at the University of Cincinnati. He lives in New Orleans with his partner, poet Kathleen Balma.